Beyond Turkey

Story by Debbie Herman
Activities by Ann D. Koffsky
Illustrated by Nancy Lane

A Thanksgiving Feast of Fun, Facts, and Activities

BARRON'S

In memory of my grandparents,
Leah and Harry Baran,
and the best Thanksgivings ever
-D.H.

For Adira Rose
-A.K.

Acknowledgments
The authors wish to thank the following people: Carolyn Freeman Travers, Research Manager at Plimoth Plantation; Susan Blei; Judy Berg; Charlotte Herman; Michael Herman; Sheila Rogers; and Brian Weiser.

All inquiries should be addressed to:
Barron's Educational Series, Inc.
250 Wireless Boulevard
Hauppauge, New York 11788
http://www.barronseduc.com

ISBN-13: 978-0-7641-3063-2
ISBN-10: 0-7641-3063-3

Library of Congress Catalog Card No. 2004057489

Herman, Debbie
   Let's celebrate: Beyond Turkey / by Debbie Herman and Ann D. Koffsky.
      p. cm. — (Let's celebrate series)
      ISBN 0-7641-3063-3
      1. Thanksgiving Day—Juvenile literature. I. Koffsky, Ann D. II. Title. III Series.

GT4975.H47 2005
394.2649—dc22

2004057489

Printed in China

9 8 7 6 5 4 3 2 1

Contents

The Story of Thanksgiving

Each year, on the fourth Thursday of November, we celebrate the holiday of Thanksgiving, joining family and friends in a feast of turkey and cranberry sauce. But how did the holiday as we know it come about, and what are we thankful for? To answer these questions we must look back at a courageous journey some ordinary people took almost 400 years ago . . .

FUN FACTS
In addition to the passengers, there were 25–30 sailors on board, and at least two dogs!

Waves crashed against the ship, tossing it up and down, and rocking it from side to side. Winds blew violently, and a crack of thunder pierced the air. Below deck, water leaked onto the passengers who huddled together, shivering, waiting for the storm to subside. One hundred and two English men, women, and children were on that ship. They had waved good-bye to family and friends one sad September day in 1620.

"Fare thee well!" they called out as the ship set sail. "Pray remember me!"

The journey would be a dangerous one, and perhaps they'd never see each other again, but they knew they had to go. Some went for religious reasons. They wanted to separate themselves from the Church of England because they disagreed with many of its ideas, but King James I would not allow it. So off to the "New World"—America—they headed, to worship as they pleased.

Other passengers were looking to make new lives for themselves. Many had been poor and hungry in England, and hoped to do better in America. Still others were looking for wealth or adventure.

Now they all sat together on the *Mayflower*, the ship that would take them to their new home.

They were ordinary people, embarking on new lives. Years later they would become known as Pilgrims—people who take a long journey.

And a long and difficult journey it was. They ate hard, dry biscuits, and cold, salty meat. Instead of water, everyone, even the children, drank beer. There was storm after storm, and many were seasick. The ship was crowded and cramped, and—because no one could bathe or wash their clothes—very smelly!

One day a man named John Howland fell overboard, but he grabbed onto a rope and was hoisted back onto the ship. Another day a baby was born. His parents named him Oceanus, because he was born on the Atlantic Ocean.

FUN FACTS
Unlike most ships, which stunk like garbage, the *Mayflower* had been used to carry barrels of wine. The scent, still lingering, helped sweeten the air.

MORE TO KNOW
Although it was a "New World" to the English, Native people had been living there for thousands of years.

Then, one joyous day, land was sighted. They had reached Cape Cod, a strip of land in what is now the state of Massachusetts.

People cheered and gave thanks. "Praise God that hath given us once again to see land."

But as they came closer to shore the land appeared desolate to them.

"There are no houses. No towns to repair to," they exclaimed, "and no one to bid us welcome."

Their only neighbors were the Wampanoag Indians, whom the Pilgrims feared.

The *Mayflower* anchored at the tip of Cape Cod, but before the people left the ship they wrote up an agreement stating that everyone must follow the rules of their new colony. This agreement became known as the Mayflower Compact.

FUN FACTS

There was also a second birth on the *Mayflower*, this time as it was anchored in the bay. The baby was named Peregrine, meaning wanderer, or pilgrim. He was the first English baby born in New England.

MORE TO KNOW

Cape Cod was not where the Pilgrims had planned to go. They had been trying to get to an area further south, by the mouth of the Hudson River, where New York City now stands, but strong winds had blown them off course.

FUN FACTS

The Pilgrims' clothing was not just black and white, as many people think, but also red, yellow, green, blue, purple, and reddish brown, and their hats and shoes didn't have buckles.

Then, at last, on November 11th, the Pilgrims stepped onto dry land. After 66 days at sea their voyage was finally over!

Many fell on their knees and prayed. Children ran. Women washed clothing. A carpenter repaired a small boat, called a shallop, which had been brought along on the *Mayflower*, and a group of men went on an exploring trip—in search of a place to build their new colony. Myles Standish, a soldier, led the way.

While waiting for a permanent place to settle, the Pilgrim women and children lived and slept on the *Mayflower*.

MORE TO KNOW

The Pilgrims arrived in Plymouth on December 16, 1620. Plymouth is in the northeastern part of the United States, which is known as New England.

For weeks the Pilgrims explored the land, but they couldn't find a suitable home for their colony. And they were running out of time.

"I pray they discover a fitting place to dwell soon," one woman told another. "Winter is coming, with much foul weather falling in."

The other woman agreed. "Our provisions are much spent. We will soon have nothing to eat. And many are becoming infected with sickness."

The Pilgrims decided to take one last exploring trip. They climbed into the shallop and sailed away. They sailed the next day, too. They rowed and rowed, fighting the winds and the waves, the snow and the rain. They continued rowing as darkness fell. That night, a strong wind blew them into a harbor. Little did they know they had found the place they would soon call home.

Upon exploring the area the next morning, the men were very pleased. Excitedly, they sailed back to the others, telling them of their discovery.

"There are running brooks of sweet, fresh water, with much good fish."

"And a great deal of land cleared for planting."

"There are forests nearby, where we can fell timber for building."

"And a great hill, on top of which we can keep watch."

" 'Tis a fine place to build our village," the others agreed.

And the *Mayflower* set sail once again—this time taking its passengers to their new home in Plymouth Harbor.

But life was difficult. Winter had arrived. The days were stormy and cold. The ground was solid as ice. The Pilgrims were exhausted, but they began to build.

As winter continued many people became ill, some from pneumonia or malnutrition. There were many deaths during that terrible winter. Only half the Pilgrims survived.

MORE TO KNOW

Fishermen, explorers, and traders had been traveling between Europe and America for years before the Pilgrims arrived.

Then one day in March, without warning, an Indian strode into their village. "Welcome Englishmen," he said. Who was this Indian, they wondered, and how did he know English? He introduced himself as Samoset. He was an Abenaki chief who had learned the language from English fishermen.

The Pilgrims gave Samoset biscuits, cheese, pudding, duck, and something to drink. They asked him many questions. Samoset told them about the neighboring Wampanoag tribes. He told them the history of the land on which they were living. It was called Patuxet, meaning "at or near the little falls." The Patuxet Wampanoag had lived there until sickness had swept across their land. Now the Pilgrims understood who had cleared their fields.

MORE TO KNOW
The mysterious sickness was smallpox. It was a disease brought over by European fishermen and explorers that came to the New World. The Patuxet had never before been exposed to such a disease, and many died.

13

Samoset left the next morning, carrying gifts he had received from the Pilgrims—a knife, a bracelet, and a ring. He returned some days later with a Wampanoag who spoke English even better than he did. His name was Tisquantum. Tisquantum was one of the few survivors of the Patuxet tribe.

Samoset and Tisquantum weren't the only people to visit the Pilgrims that day. Chief Massasoit, a leader of the Wampanoag, joined them as well, bringing sixty men with him.

After exchanging greetings and gifts, the Pilgrims and Wampanoag signed a peace treaty, with Tisquantum serving as their translator.

"We shall live together in peace," they agreed, "and if one people shall suffer attack, the other shall come to its aid."

The Pilgrims said good-bye to their Wampanoag neighbors, but Tisquantum stayed on and lived with the Pilgrims for the rest of his life. He became known as Squanto.

MORE TO KNOW
The peace between the Pilgrims and the Wampanoag lasted over fifty years.

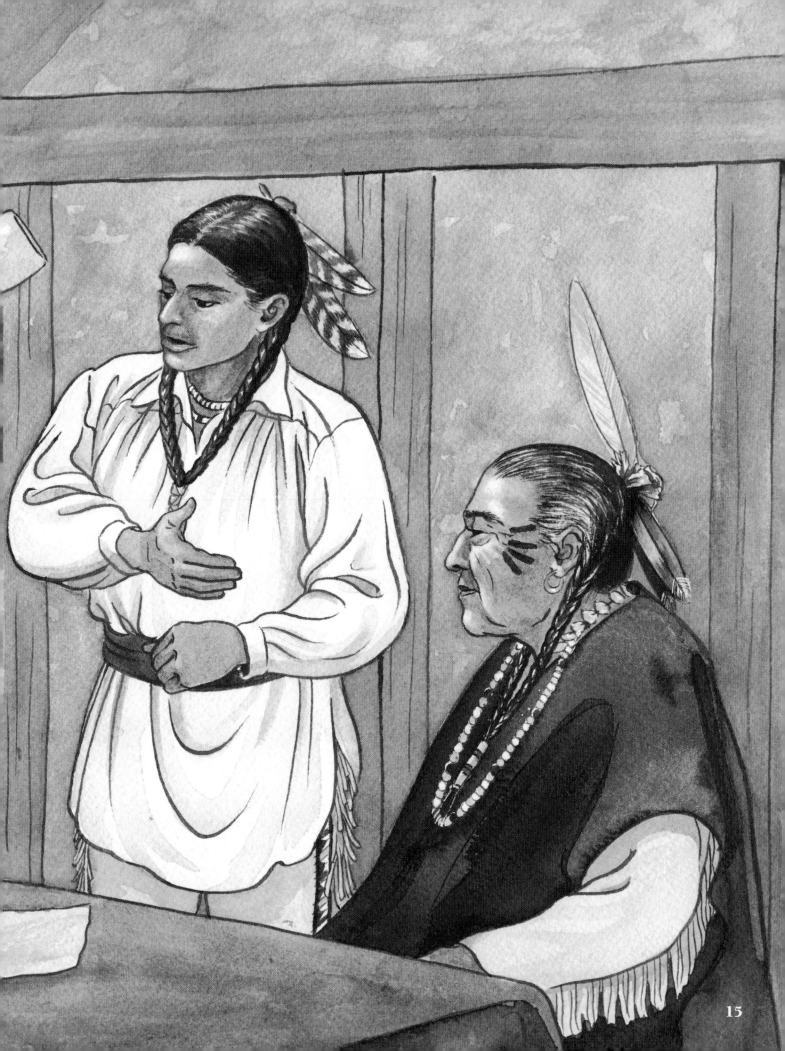

Squanto was a great help to the Pilgrims. He showed them how to plant corn, using herring as fertilizer. He taught them how to dig for clams and catch eels with their bare hands. Squanto pointed out which plants were edible and which were poisonous. He showed them where the best berries grew. Squanto also acted as their guide and their interpreter.

Everyone worked hard that spring, planting, hunting, fishing, and building. The children worked hard too. They had many jobs, including gathering mussels and clams, guarding cornfields from animals, and making mattresses by filling linen bags with straw or feathers.

FUN FACTS
While many Pilgrims had traditional names like John or Mary, others had names like Love, Humility, and Remember!

On April 5, 1621, the *Mayflower* and its crew returned to England, but the Pilgrims remained.

Spring turned into summer, and summer to fall. Now it was harvest time. The ripened crops were gathered to eat and to store away for winter. The harvest was a good one. There were many different fruits and vegetables, including corn, pumpkins, and gooseberries. There was plenty of fish and meat. Food was dried and pickled, to last through the winter. The future looked hopeful. The Pilgrims wanted to celebrate their plentiful harvest, as they had done back in England.

"Let us prepare a goodly feast to celebrate our harvest," announced William Bradford, the governor of Plymouth.

MORE TO KNOW
The first governor of Plymouth was John Carver. He died that winter, and William Bradford took over.

To prepare, men hunted duck, wild turkey, and geese. Others fished for cod, bass, and eel. When the feast began in the fall of 1621, fifty-two Pilgrims gathered together to eat and celebrate. There were no forks on the table, because the English in those days ate with their hands! They had big cloth napkins to wipe their hands, and they ate out of wooden plates, called trenchers.

Massasoit joined them, bringing along some Wampanoag friends—ninety of them! They went into the forest, and returned with five deer to add to the feast.

FUN FACTS

In the 1700s, Benjamin Franklin wanted to make the wild turkey, and not the bald eagle, the national bird of the United States.

FUN FACTS
While the Pilgrims might have had cranberries and pumpkins at their harvest feast, they did not have cranberry sauce or pumpkin pie, and while they probably did serve turkey, it was only one of many foods.

MORE TO KNOW
Plymouth was the second permanent English settlement in the New World (Jamestown, Virginia was the first). It, along with the many others that followed, eventually became the United States of America.

Aside from eating and drinking, adults and children played games. There were foot races and jumping contests. Adults played tug-of-war. Men had log-throwing contests. The Pilgrims sang songs from the Bible and English folk songs. Myles Standish led the Pilgrim men in a military parade, where they marched to a drum and fired their muskets. The Wampanoag shot their arrows, and entertained the crowd with dancing. The feast lasted for three days!

MORE TO KNOW
America's growth unfortunately also led to the Native people's loss of land and way of life.

Things were looking better for the Pilgrims. Some of their houses had already been completed. They were healthier now, and had food for the winter. They were in a land where they could practice their religion, and they were at peace with their Wampanoag neighbors. But most of all they had hope that their little colony would survive and grow. And it did.

Thanksgiving today is a combination of two customs—Puritan thanksgiving days and English harvest festivals. Thanksgiving days were religious holidays established as days of thanks to God when especially good things happened, and were spent in prayer. Harvest festivals were secular (nonreligious) holidays, celebrated with feasting, after a good harvest.

Thanksgiving Days were declared during and after the birth of America, with different colonies, states, and territories celebrating them on and off at different times. In the 1800s, a writer and editor named Sara Josepha Hale urged American leaders to make Thanksgiving a yearly holiday, celebrated by the entire country. In 1863 President Lincoln proclaimed Thanksgiving Day a national holiday, to be celebrated from that day forward.

FUN FACTS

You can experience what life was like for the Pilgrims by visiting Plimoth Plantation, a living history museum in Plymouth, Massachusetts, where "interpreters" re-create life in Plymouth by dressing, speaking, and acting like the Pilgrims did. You can also climb aboard a reproduction of the *Mayflower*!

In the mid 1800s, and even more so in the 1900s, people recalled the story of the 1621 harvest feast, which they incorrectly believed to be "the first Thanksgiving," and linked it to their own Thanksgiving celebration. As America continued to grow, with immigrants coming from many different countries, this image of two very different cultures feasting together seemed the perfect symbol for the American holiday. The story of the Plymouth Pilgrims and their Wampanoag neighbors has been closely connected to our Thanksgiving holiday ever since.

Activity Section

by Ann D. Koffsky

A note to kids and their parents: Many of these crafts involve materials that should only be handled with adult supervision. This includes scissors and especially cooking utensils. Please exercise caution, and make this Thanksgiving a happy and a safe holiday! Each activity has a turkey next to its name. The more turkeys pictured, the more complex the activity (1 is easiest, 4 is hardest).

For the Table

Stuff the Charity Turkey!

Want to emphasize the "giving" in Thanksgiving? Add this turkey centerpiece to your table.

You will need:

Brown, yellow, and orange construction paper	2 Googly eyes	Marker
1 Candy corn	Tracing paper	Feathers
1 Red balloon	1 Decorative paper plate	Stapler
	1 Empty, clean oatmeal container	Masking Tape

1. Cover the oatmeal container and lid with the brown construction paper, and glue in place. Cover the two pieces of the container separately so that the lid can still come on and off.

2. Glue feathers to both sides of the plate in a circle so that the tips of the feathers all point to a spot just below the center of the plate. Decorate the oatmeal container with feathers.

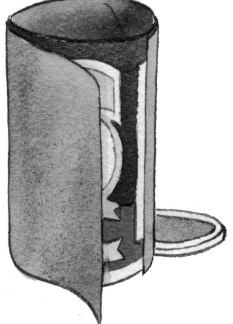

3. To make the turkey's head and feet, trace the templates at right onto tracing paper.

4. Tape the tracing paper to your orange construction paper. Cutting along the lines, cut out the feet and head.

5. Assemble the turkey: Have a grown-up staple the bottom of the plate to the back of the container. Then, fold the turkey's neck along the dashed line. Tape the folded portion to the container, and bend the turkey's neck outward. Glue more feathers on the neck and container to cover up the tape.

6. To make your candy corn beak, fold the turkey's beak along the solid line. Glue the candy corn bottom onto the folded triangle.

7. Tape the feet to the bottom of the container.

8. Glue the googly eyes in place. Create the wattle by gluing the red balloon onto the turkey's neck.

9. Remove the cover of the oatmeal container. Cut out a quarter-sized rectangular hole in the center of the lid.

10. Use a marker to write around the top of the lid, "Help stuff the Turkey! Stuffing will be donated to_____." Fill in the blank with the charity organization of your choice.

27

Ti Pi & Wetu Napkin Ring Place Cards

Use some of the many different early Native American homes as templates for napkin ring place cards at your table.

You will need:
Colored toothpicks
1 Empty paper towel roll
1 Sheet of patterned contact paper
2 Sheets of differently colored pieces of cardstock paper

Optional: Photos of the people who will be at the Thanksgiving table
Colored markers
Tracing paper

Ti Pi

1. Cover the paper towel roll with the contact paper.
2. Cut the roll into 3/4-inch-wide rings.
3. To make a ti pi napkin ring, trace the template below onto tracing paper.

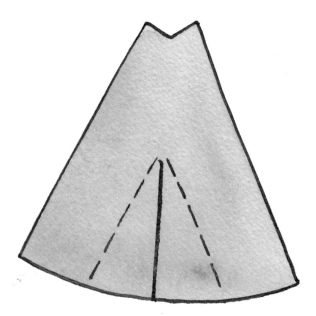

4. Tape the tracing paper to one sheet of the cardstock paper.
5. Hold the two pieces of cardstock paper together, and cut out the ti pi. Do not cut out the door.
6. Put down the bottom layer of cardstock paper. Now cut along the center line and make a door in just the top cardstock paper ti pi. Fold along the dotted lines to open it.

7. Glue the three toothpicks to the bottom ti pi as shown.

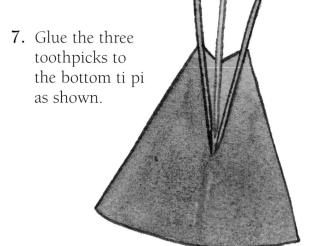

8. Glue the ti pi with the cutout door on top of the bottom layer. Be sure to seal all around the edges. Make sure the door stays open and does not get glued shut.

Wetu

1. Cover the paper towel roll with the contact paper.
2. Cut the roll into 3/4-inch-wide rings.
3. To make a wetu napkin ring, trace the template at right onto tracing paper.
4. Tape the tracing paper to one sheet of the cardstock paper.
5. Hold the two pieces of cardstock paper together, and cut out the wetu. Do not cut out the door.
6. Put down the bottom layer of paper. Cut along the solid line of the door. Fold along the dotted line.
7. With a crayon or marker, draw the lines of the wetu as shown.
8. Snap 3 toothpicks in half (you may need a grown-up to help you).
9. Glue the toothpicks onto the wetu as shown.
10. Glue the top layer of cardstock to the bottom layer. Make sure the door stays open and does not get glued shut.

For Both Ti Pi & Wetu

After the glue dries, write the names of your guests inside the doors, onto the bottom layers. If you have photos, you can cut out the faces of your guests and glue them inside the door, too.

Then, glue the ti pis and wetus to the sides of the rings. Roll up your dinner napkins and slip one inside each ring. Use the rings as place cards.

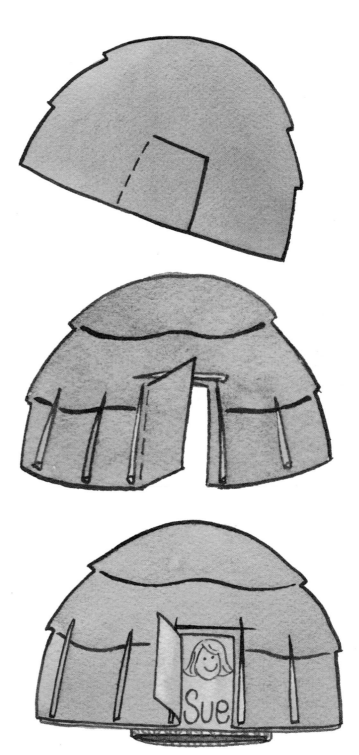

Balloon Bouquet

These balloons do double duty: They make a fun arrangement for your table, and a great addition to your Thanskgiving parade on page 44.

You will need:

5 Balloons in any light colors (do not use black or other very dark colors). They should not be blown up.

5 Coat hangers with cardboard bottoms

Pen

Clear tape

Ribbon

A 2-liter plastic soda bottle

Glue

Tissue paper

1. Think of 5 things that you are thankful for. With the pen, write a word for them onto each uninflated balloon.

2. Blow up your balloons and tie them. (You might need a grown-up to help you.) Watch what happens to the words as the balloons blow up!

3. Have an adult help you remove the cardboard dowels from the coat hangers. Cut the ends off some of them with sharp scissors so that they are each different lengths.

4. Decorate the dowels by wrapping the ribbons around them as shown. Tape with clear tape to hold in place.

5. Tape the bottom of each balloon to the end of a dowel.
6. Remove the label from the soda bottle (soaking it in warm water can make this easier).
7. Cut the bottle in half. Discard the top.
8. Cut or tear the tissue paper into many pieces.
9. Dip the tissue pieces in glue, and paste to the soda bottle. Cover most of the soda bottle with layers of the tissue pieces.
10. When the glue has dried, fold remaining large sheets of tissue paper inside the bottle, and let them drape over the top of the bottle to cover the edges.
11. Arrange the balloon sticks inside the bottle, and display your thankful balloon bouquet. If the bottle is tipping, weight the bottom with rocks from your nature walk on page 48.

31

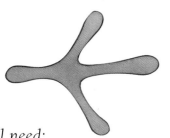

Turkey Tracks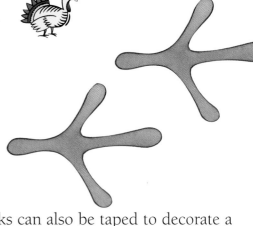

A fun and easy decoration.

You will need:
Pencil
Tracing paper
Masking tape that isn't
   too sticky

Scissors
Many sheets of the same
   color construction paper

1. Trace the turkey footprints on the opposite page onto the tracing paper.
2. Tape the tracing to your construction paper.
3. Take several sheets of paper together. Use the template as a guide, and cut out several "tracks" at once. Repeat for as many tracks as you'll need.
4. To make tape circles for the bottom of each footprint, just tear off a piece of masking tape, and attach the two ends. (You may need more than one tape circle for each footprint.)
5. Tape the turkey footprints around your home. You can have turkey trails on the floor: one color trail could lead your guests from the front door to where they should put their coats. A different color trail of tracks could lead them to the dinner table.

Turkey tracks can also be taped to decorate a paper tablecloth, a wall—even the ceiling!

Tip: Make your tape less sticky so that it can easily be removed from floors or walls. Just line strips of the tape onto any kind of material, like a shirt or blanket. Then, peel the strips off, and use.

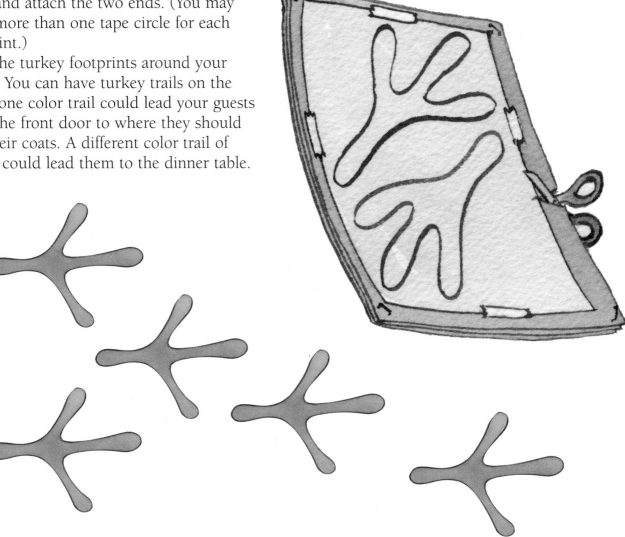

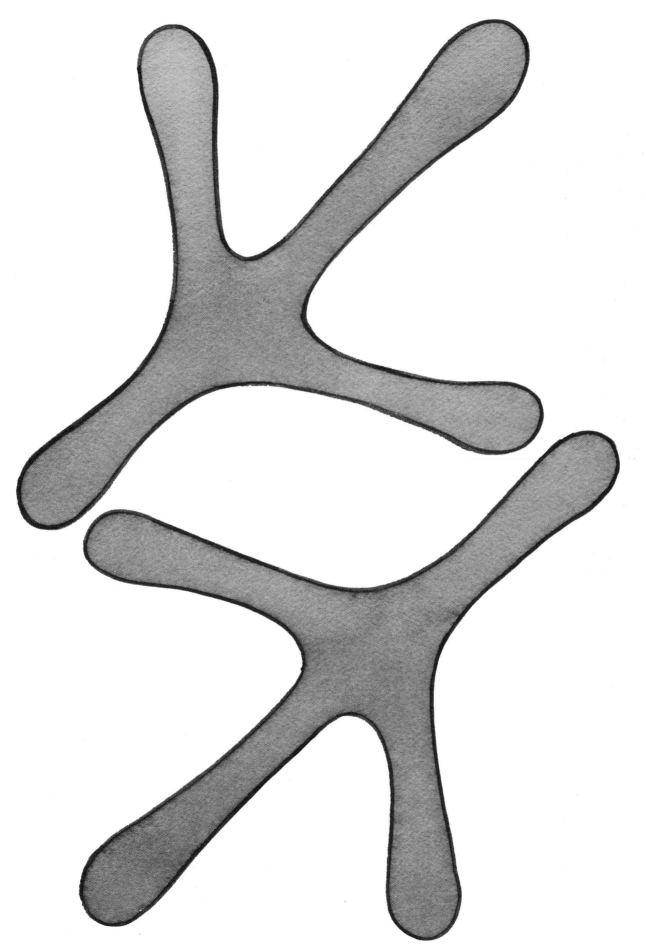

33

Thanks for Coming!

This charming door decoration can be put on the outside of your front door to welcome guests as they arrive, or on the inside to wish them well as they leave.

You will need:

Flat leaves from your nature walk (see page 48)
White crayons
10 × 13 piece of white craft paper
1 Large sheet of colored paper or posterboard
   that is slightly larger than the white paper
1 5 × 7 piece of colored paper

Glue or glue stick
Large foam brush
Water
Watercolor paints
Hole puncher
Ribbon

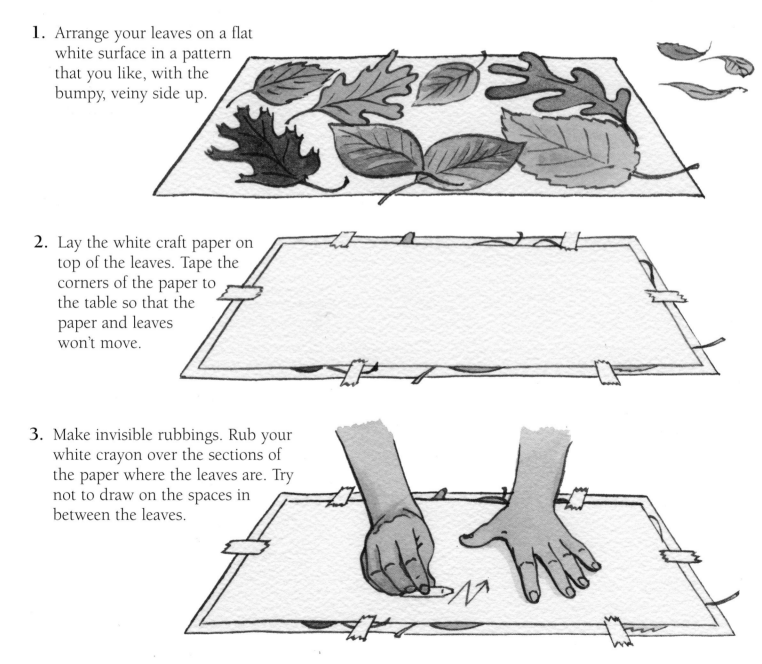

1. Arrange your leaves on a flat white surface in a pattern that you like, with the bumpy, veiny side up.

2. Lay the white craft paper on top of the leaves. Tape the corners of the paper to the table so that the paper and leaves won't move.

3. Make invisible rubbings. Rub your white crayon over the sections of the paper where the leaves are. Try not to draw on the spaces in between the leaves.

4. Dip your paintbrush in the watercolor paint, and paint over the entire surface of the paper. Your leaves should now appear on the paper!

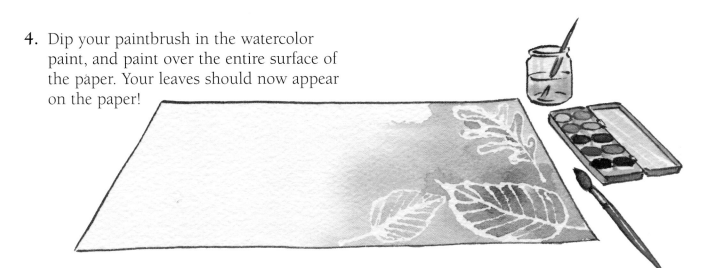

5. Put the painting aside to dry.
6. Take the smaller, 5 × 7 piece of paper, and write the message "Thanks for Coming!" You can decorate the letters any way you like.

7. Mount the leaf painting to the center of the larger piece of colored paper. Then, glue the smaller "Thanks" paper to the center of the leaf painting.
8. Punch two holes in the top of the large colored paper. Thread ribbon through the hole and tie. Hang by the ribbon on your door.

Football Remote Control Holder

Many a Thanksgiving dinner ends with everyone watching a football game on TV. Here's a craft that football fans will be thankful for!

You will need:

1 Half-gallon cardboard milk container, empty and washed

2 One-quart cardboard milk containers, empty and washed

Green construction paper

Black construction paper

Glue

A white oil pastel crayon or a white colored pencil

A good scissor that can cut through cardboard

1. Cut the tops off of each of the milk containers, so that the remaining bottoms are 5-1/2 inches tall.

3. Cover the interior of the container with black paper. Cover the pieces of the quart containers that you will be using in black construction paper.

4. Insert the two larger pieces of the quart containers into the half-gallon container as shown. Have a grown-up staple the pieces together.

2. Cut the quart bottoms lengthwise, so that the larger pieces are just a little bigger than half the container.

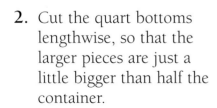

5. Cover three sides of the outside of the half-gallon container with green construction paper. Cover the fourth side with black construction paper.
6. Draw a football field onto the green paper with the white crayon or pencil.
7. In each of the end zones, write the name of your favorite team. Or you can write your family name (such as Team Koffsky! or Team Herman!).
8. This Thanksgiving, take a photo of everyone watching TV. Paste it to the center of the fourth side of the holder. Using the white crayon or marker, write a caption underneath saying, "Thanksgiving, 200_" (fill in the right year).

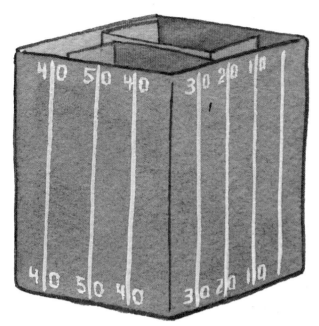

Food (Desserts)
Mayflower Cupcake

For each cupcake, you will need:

2 Colored toothpicks
1 Candy fruit slice
2 Mini candy fish

1 Fruit rollup
Ocean frosting
    (see recipe at right)

Ocean Frosting

1 Cup softened butter (2 sticks)
1 Tsp. vanilla
3 Tbs. of milk (or more, if needed)
1 Lb. box confectioners sugar
1/2 Tsp. almond extract
Blue food coloring

1. Ask an adult to bake cupcakes for this project. Let cool.
2. Frost your cupcakes with the blue icing. Then, dip a plastic knife into the remaining white icing, and swirl it into the blue to create an ocean frosting.
3. Spear two toothpicks all the way through the candy fruit slice as shown (this will be your boat). They should stick out just a little bit from the bottom.
4. Cut out small shapes of fruit rollup. Spear the rollup shapes at the top and bottom with the toothpicks (see picture).
5. Put the boat into the blue frosting deep enough so the toothpicks pierce the cupcake and hold the boat in place.
6. Cut off the head of the two candy fish and stick into frosting near the front of the boat, so that it looks like they are peeking out of the water to look at the *Mayflower*.

1. Mix all the ingredients, except for the food coloring, together.
2. Add more milk as needed to make the consistancy of the icing easy to spread.
3. Split the frosting into two bowls, with most of the frosting in one bowl. Add a few drops of the blue food coloring to the larger batch of frosting and mix well. Leave the remaining frosting white, and swirl in later.

Fun Idea: Scatter the extra candy fish on the platter from which you serve the cupcakes.

Tasty Pilgrim Hats

You will need:
Miniature Reese's Peanut Butter Cup
Chocolate sandwich cookie
Yellow jelly bean or candy corn
Yellow or orange fruit rollup
Chocolate frosting

1. Remove the foil from the peanut butter cup.
2. Separate the two halves of the sandwich cookies. To make a Pilgrim hat, you will only need the cookie half that doesn't have the icing on it, so feel free to eat up the side that does!
3. Put a small spoon of frosting in the center of the plain cookie half.
4. Turn the peanut butter cup upside-down, and stick to the center of the cookie circle.
5. Frost over the entire cookie and peanut butter cup.
6. With a plastic knife, slice a thin strip of the fruit rollup and wrap it around the base of the peanut butter cup to look like a band around the hat.

7. Dip the yellow jelly bean into the frosting, and stick to the fruit rollup so it looks like the buckle on the hat. Or, slice off the yellow part of a candy corn, dip it in the frosting, and use that as the buckle instead.

Fun Idea: Pilgrim hats could also be made by cutting off the stump of a cupcake and attaching it with frosting to a larger round cookie. Frost completely with chocolate frosting. Then add the candy and fruit rollup. Add either kind of hat to a larger cake as a decoration.

Red, White, and Blue Fruit Salad

Since many people are thankful for this country, add the flag's colors to your Thanksgiving table.

Strawberries	Blueberries
Bananas	Plastic knife

1. Wash the strawberries and blueberries in the sink. Lay them on a paper towel and pat dry.
2. Cut the green stems off the strawberries. Peel the bananas.
3. Slice the strawberries and bananas. Toss it all into a glass or clear plastic bowl.

Easy Cranberry Sauce

You will need:
2 Cups sugar   2 Cups water
1 Lb. bag cranberries

Put water and sugar into a pot, and bring to a boil.
Add the cranberries, and cook until tender.

Very Easy Cranberry Sauce

You will need:
1 Can wholeberry cranberries   1 Can crushed pineapple   1 Can mandarin oranges drained
1 Cup chopped pecans

Open cans. Dump all ingredients into a bowl. Mix and serve.

Pumpkin-Cranberry Muffins

You will need:
1 Can pumpkin (15 oz)   3 Cups flour   1 Tsp. baking soda
3 Cups sugar   1-1/2 Tsp. cinnamon   3 Eggs
1 Cup oil   1/2 Tsp. baking powder   1 Lb. bag fresh cranberries

1. Mix all of the ingredients together, except
   for the cranberries.
2. Then, mix in the cranberries.
3. Grease tins.
4. Fill each cup halfway with batter.
   Put in oven on 350° for
   30 minutes.

Makes 44 muffins.

Horn of Plenty

A horn of plenty is a symbol of the harvest, and usually holds fruits and vegetables.
So why not use fruits and vegetables to decorate them?

You will need:

Large, brown paper lunch bags
Paper plates
Orange, yellow, and red Tempera paint

An apple, a potato, a pepper and other
vegetables to experiment with

You might want to protect your work area by laying down some newspaper first.

1. Pour the different colored paints onto paper plates.
2. Slice the apple and potato in half (you might want to slice
   the apple horizontally, so that you can see the "star" inside).
   Cut a ring of the pepper so that it looks a little bit
   like a flower. You will use
   these to "stamp" your bag.

3. Decorate your bags by dipping your fruits and vegetables into the paints and stamping them
   onto the bag. Create patterns, stripes—whatever you like.
4. Wait for one side to dry, then flip the bag and do the next side. Don't forget to decorate
   the sides, too.
5. Make the bags into horns of plenty. First, fold down the tops of the bag. Then, twist
   the bottoms of the bag to form a cone shape.
6. Fill with the fruits, and lay it on its side.
   Add it to your dessert table, or use as a
   centerpiece.

Fun Idea: To create an
interesting pattern on
your bags, dip an
ear of corn into
the paint and
roll it all
around the
paper.

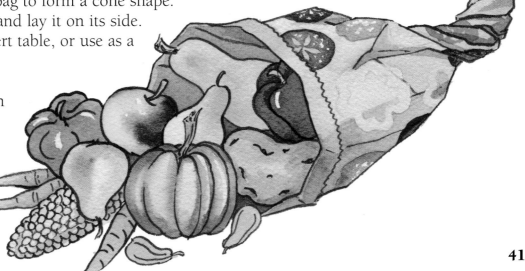

Inside Game

Mayflower Maze Race

Race to get your ship to the New World first.

Maze

The real Pilgrims on the Mayflower faced many obstacles on their trip to the New World, such as illness, overcrowding, storms, and hunger. Make these obstacles for your own ship to navigate around.

You will need:

Tracing paper   Tape/glue
Construction paper   Marker
A long rectangle aluminum   Scissors
   foil pan   Pencil

1. With a pencil, trace each of the "obstacle" pictures onto tracing paper.
2. Tape the tracing paper to pieces of construction paper, and use them as guides to cut out each obstacle from the construction paper. Discard the tracing paper.
3. Tape or glue the obstacles to the bottom of your pan. Make sure to leave space between the obstacles.
4. With a marker, write "Old World— England" on one end of your pan, and "New World—Plymouth Rock" on the other end. Your maze is now ready for your ship.

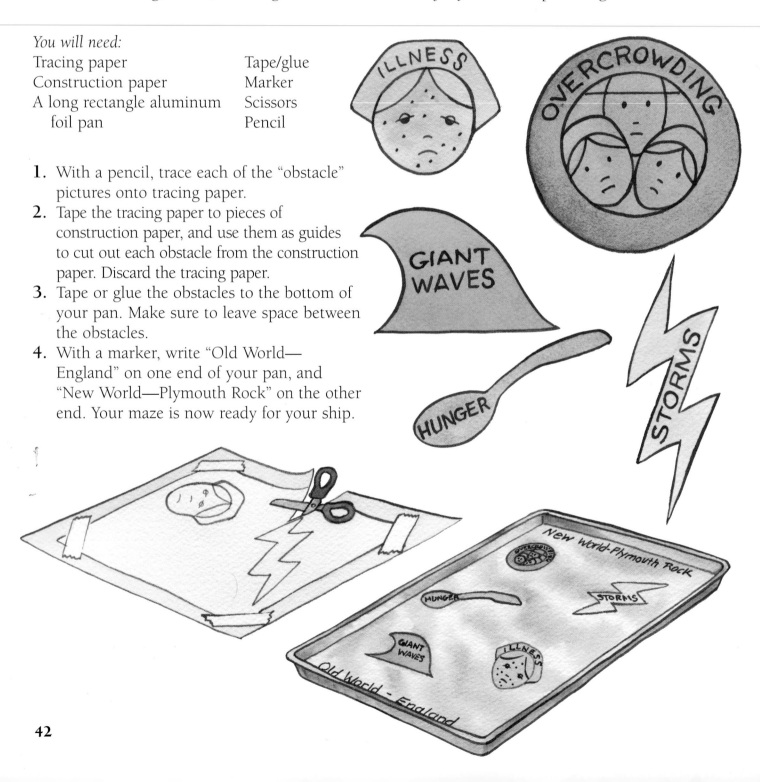

Ship Magnets

You will need:
A sheet of red, white, and blue craft foam
2 Colored toothpicks
Two 1/2-inch round super-strong ceramic magnets

Tracing paper
Pencil
Tacky craft glue

1. Trace the templates below onto the tracing paper. Trace the boat bottom twice.
2. Tape the sail template to the white craft foam. Tape the boat bottoms to the red craft foam. Tape the water template to the blue craft foam.
3. Using the tracings as guides, cut out each shape from the craft foam.
4. Thread two white sails onto each toothpick as shown.
5. Glue the bottom of the toothpicks on top of the first boat bottom.
6. Glue the second boat bottom on top of the first. This will sandwich the bottoms of the toothpicks in place.
7. Glue the water on top of the boat.
8. Glue the magnet to the back of the boat
9. With a pen, write the word *Mayflower* across the boat.

To Play:
Place the boat magnet in the foil pan, where it says "Old World." Holding your pan with one hand, use your second hand to hold the second magnet. Hold it directly under your ship. As you move the second magnet, your boat will move too! Get your *Mayflower* from the Old World to Plymouth Rock in the New World without hitting any of the obstacles. Ready? Go!

Play alone against a kitchen timer to see how fast you can make the crossing. Or, if you want to race against a friend, make twice as many of everything described above.

Fun Idea: When you're done with the game, use the boats as refrigerator magnets.

Inside or Outside Game

Parade

The Native Americans taught the Pilgrims how to respect and cultivate the Earth. Today, one of the best ways to cherish the Earth is to take care of it by reusing and recycling. Here is one idea for reusing some homemade items to create your own Thanksgiving parade. Look around your home for other recyclables that you can turn into musical instruments.

Noisemaker 1

Did you make an apple or pumpkin pie for dinner? Remember to set aside the seeds to make this noisemaker.

You will need:
2 Paper plates   Paint
Stapler   1 Apple

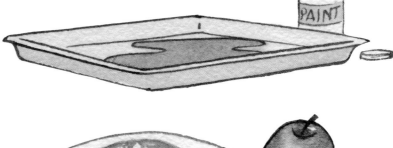

1. Have a grown-up slice an apple in half, lengthwise. What do you see inside?
2. Dip the apple in paint, and use it as a stamp to decorate the bottom sides of the two paper plates.
3. Place the pumpkin and/or apple seeds on one plate. Then, ask a grown-up to staple the two plates together so that you can see the decorations. The seeds should be sealed inside.
4. To put on a Thanksgiving parade, use this noisemaker and the ballons from page 30.

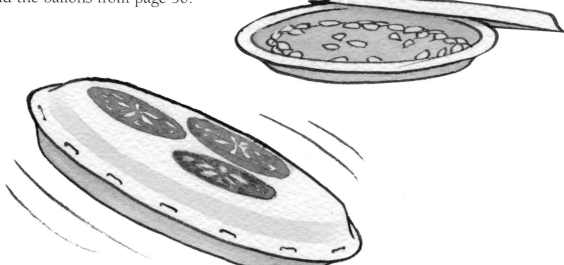

Noisemaker 2

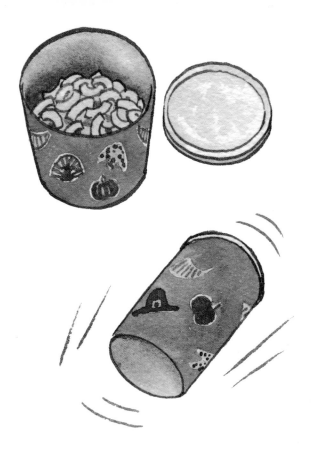

You will need:
Coffee can
Uncooked pasta, such as macaroni or shells
Construction paper
Stickers/markers/glitter
Glue

1. Glue construction paper to the coffee can to cover.
2. Decorate the can with stickers.
3. Fill the can 1/4 of the way with the dry pasta.
4. Put the lid on the can, and shake, shake, shake!

Baton

You will need:
An empty gift wrap roll   Paint
Scotch tape   Stickers
Streamers

1. Paint the gift wrap roll and let dry.
2. Tape streamers to both ends of the roll, and twirl away!

Collect all your parade props, including the balloon sticks from your balloon bouquet on page 30, and put on a parade! March to a tape of marching music, or just make your own.

Drum

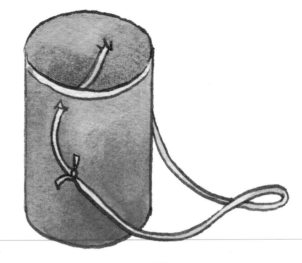

You will need:
An iced tea container or oatmeal container
30-inch piece of elastic
Construction paper
Square piece of felt large enough to cover the top of your
    container
Rubber band

1. Cover the can with the construction paper.
2. To create a strap to carry the drum by in the parade, have a grown-up pierce two holes on opposite sides of the can.
3. Thread the elastic through the two holes, and tie the ends together.
4. Place the lid on top of the can. Cover the lid with the felt square, and attach the felt to the can with a rubber band.
5. Beat your new drum with your hands or with a spoon.

Fun Idea: The best and easiest drums are empty pots with wooden spoons. Two similarly sized pot lids are great (noisy!) cymbals.

Outside Games

Dessert Harvest

This is a great game for a big group of kids to play.

You will need:

Lots of two types of candy that come individually wrapped, like hard candies. You can also use peanuts and walnuts, still in their shells. (Be sure to check that none of the players have nut allergies!)

3 paper bags
If the weather isn't too cold, you can do this in an outside yard. A large indoor area, like a basement, will also work.

To Play:

1. Have a grown-up hide lots of each type of candy around the basement or yard. If there are still leaves on the ground, he or she can hide them under and around leaves.
2. Divide the kids into two teams with a grab bag. Put as many pieces of the two candies as there are kids into the first bag. For example, if there are 10 kids, put 5 red candies and 5 yellow candies in the bag. Have each kid take a turn picking a candy from the bag. Whichever candy they pick is the team they're on.
3. Have everyone go outside or into the basement. Put one bag on one side of the lawn (or basement) and one bag on the other. Assign a team to each bag. Each team has to get their own kind of candy into their bag. They can't touch the second kind of candy. Have a grown-up yell, "On your mark. Get set. Go!"

4. When all the candy has been collected, empty the bags into piles on the table.
5. Make the bags into horns of plenty. First, fold down the tops of the bag. Then, twist the bottoms of the bag to form a cone shape.
6. Put the piles of candy back inside the bags, and lay them on their sides on the dessert table to serve.

Nature Walk

Go on a fall nature walk and collect things with your feet!

Put on your shoes and socks. Then, take a pair of a grown-up's old socks and pull them over your shoes. Go for a nature walk around your home, or in a park. When you're done, see what stuck to your socks. Glue the ones you like to a piece of paper, and hang the paper in your home as a nature collage.

Use your hands on the nature walk to collect some leaves for the projects on page 34 (door sign) and rocks for the balloon bouquet on page 30.

Travel Games

If you're not hosting Thanksgiving dinner this year, you're probably one of the thousands of guests who will be traveling by car to their hosts to celebrate. Here are some fun games to keep you busy on the road.

Turkey Twenty

Play twenty questions, with a turkey twist. The first person thinks of something having to do with Thanksgiving. Everyone else gets to ask that person up to 20 yes or no questions to figure out what they're thinking of.

Thanksgiving Dinner

The first person finishes the sentence "At Thanksgiving dinner, I like to eat…." Let's say they choose "Turkey." The second person then repeats the same sentence, "At Thanksgiving dinner, I like to eat Turkey and …" adding one food. The third person now needs to remember the first two foods, and add a third. Go around the car, adding one food each turn until you can't remember all the foods!

Letter License Plate

Choose a simple Thanksgiving word, and see who can first find the letters to spell it. Look for the letters on license plates, or on street and traffic signs. Make sure to find the letters in the correct order. Here are some words to start with: turkey, Pilgrim, corn, America, ship, harvest.